# EASY FLAME SOLOS

CW01022545

### by
### Mel Agen

**Online Audio**    www.melbay.com/96623BCDEB

---

## Book & Audio Contents

1 2 3 4 5 6 7 8 9 0

© 1998 BY MEL BAY PUBLICATIONS, INC., PACIFIC, MO 63069.
ALL RIGHTS RESERVED. INTERNATIONAL COPYRIGHT SECURED. B.M.I. MADE AND PRINTED IN U.S.A.

**Visit us on the Web at http://www.melbay.com — E-mail us at email@melbay.com**

**MEL BAY** ®

# Gypsy Style Flamenco

What is it? It is music played on the guitar using many different variations and patterns to develop a melody. To see how it is developed let's go back and follow Great-great-grandfather Mercer on his musical journeys.

He was born in Flandre, a small country between France and Belgium. From the name Flandre comes the word Flemish. From the word Flemish comes the word Flamenco. Now the little country of Flandre had two parts: the east side called Oriental Flandre and the west side called Occidental Flandre. Great-great-grandfather was from the west side and great-great-grandmother was from the east side. She played classical guitar; he played flamenco. The two styles have many things in common: tremolos, picados, arpeggios, that are played with the right hand.

At each inn they played at, he would start the program. He would start most pieces by playing a rasqueado. The rasqueado is a very loud introduction to a melody, using the chord cycle or a part of it by fanning or scratching (ras) the fingers of the right hand in intricate patterns across the strings. He did this to turn attention to his playing as there was much conversation and noise in the inns where they played.

He would play for 15 minutes and then she would play for 15 minutes. No one turned away when she played those melodic classical pieces and her variations on local and well-known folk songs. Then he would play flamenco for another 15 minutes before they took a short break; then they would start over, playing different pieces.

It was not always easy to make a living in Flandre as there were many good guitarists in Flandre, east and west. Also the eastern and western melodies were shared by all. Flandre was crowded in those days so they decided to travel. They had two claims to the heritage of the name "Gypsy," as the name means wanderer. Both their Oriental and Occidental ancestors wandered to Flandre and now they were wandering away.

While wandering through France, they found they could do better if they worked only the inns that served food as well as ale.

In southern France they stopped for a time in the horse and cattle country. Many of their friends from Flandre, who also played and danced, had wandered in this direction too. They were appreciated in this area for their music but many wanted to push on to Spain as they heard of great singers and guitarists in Spain. Somehow they felt in their hearts that they were going home.

The gypsies and musicians of Spain liked what they heard of the music each played. Between them, they created the great pieces of music that are now known all over the world as "flamenco." However, each played just a little differently.

This book is dedicated to the student of the guitar who wants to play flamenco guitar correctly in the shortest possible time. This book will show you the most used techniques and exactly how they are played. Each example will be as simple as possible yet melodic in its content.

Each "variation" on the flamenco guitar is called a "falseta," so it is readily seen that a melody could be varied in many different ways. A simple melody could be made to sound very complicated, but the guitarist, because he knows the techniques, would have no difficulty. Guitarists, like yourself, will get a great amount of satisfaction in using these techniques.

The lessons will progress from the most simple, on to the more complex, and will follow in logical sequence. Each melody should be memorized and added to your "repertoire." If you are a newcomer to the art, each page should be studied about one week to get the best results.

---

### Note to the Students of Flamenco

It is common practice in club and concert work to put flamenco pieces of the same name and key from several different books in sequence to extend the pieces.

Mel Agen

---

# Study 1

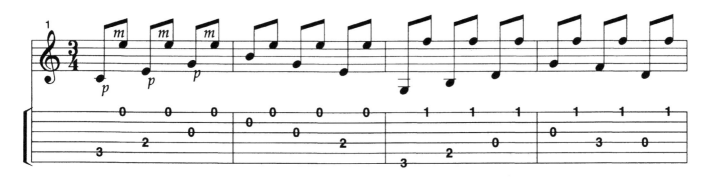

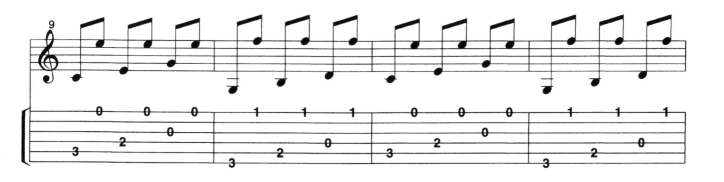

# Study 2

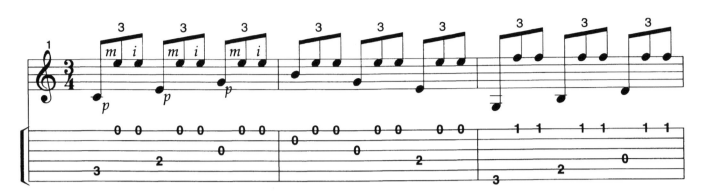

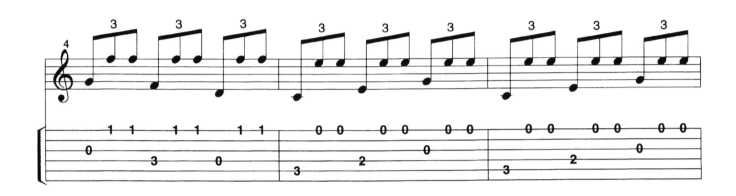

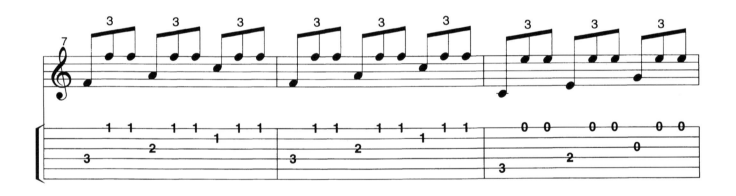

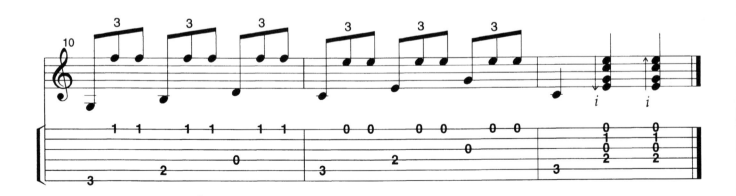

# Study 3

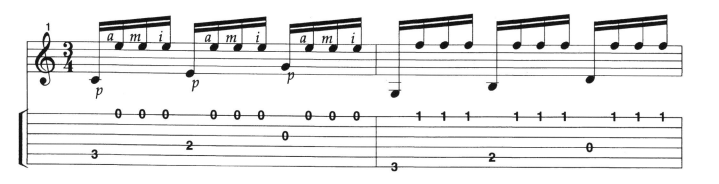

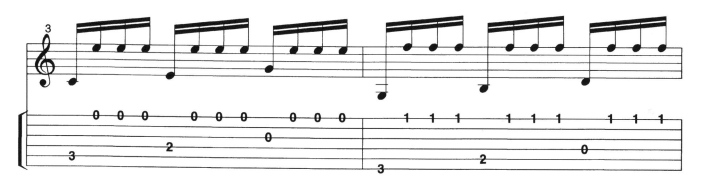

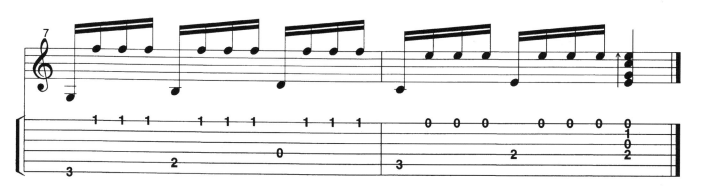

# Study 4

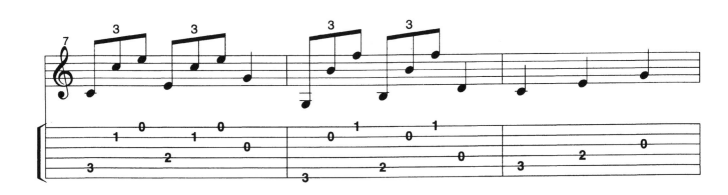

# Study 5
## Melody in A Minor

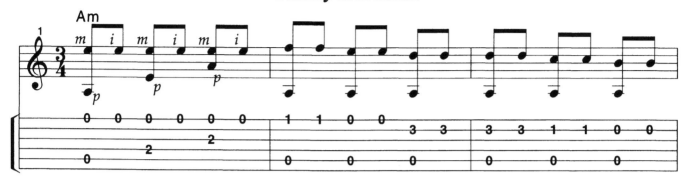

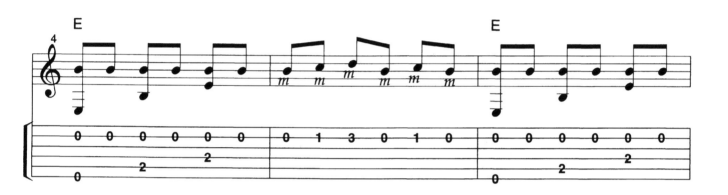

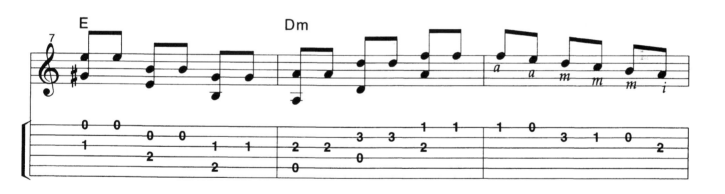

# Study 6
## Melody in A Minor

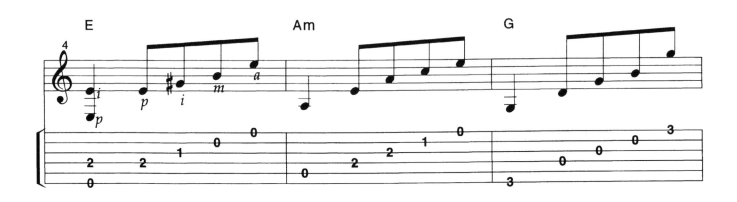

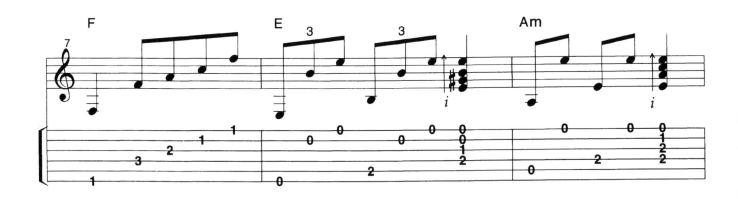

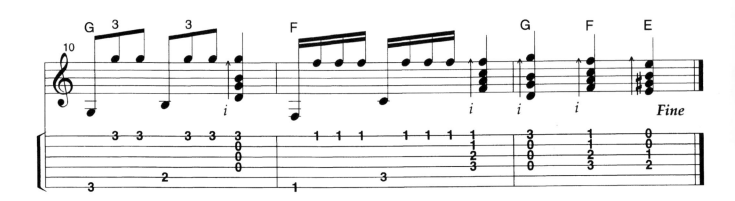

# Study 7
## Melody in A Minor

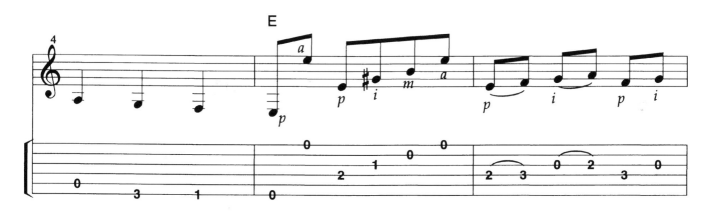

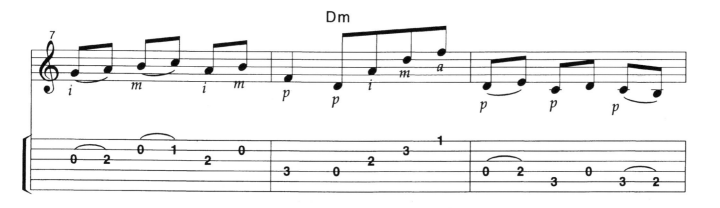

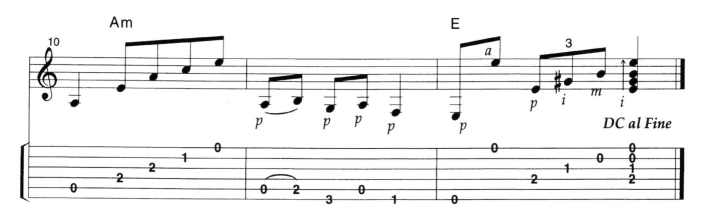

# Study 8

# In Memory of Carlos

Bend B flat notes slightly
in the picado indicated by bird's eye.

Mel Agen

Chords are held down in measures 13-15.
Only the basses change.

Chords are held down in measures 41-43.
Only the basses change.

# Gypsy Fandango

*Mel Agen*

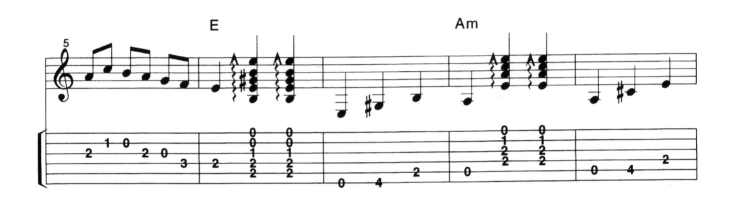

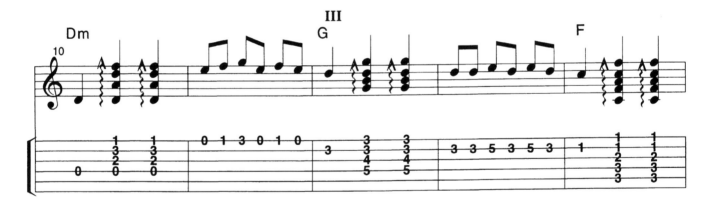

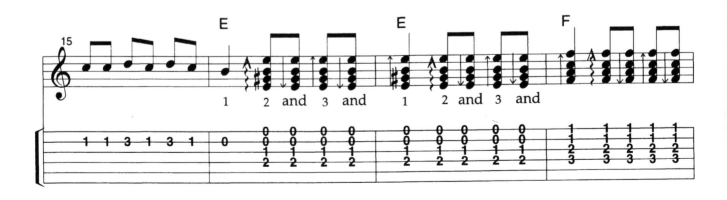

An H over a chord means it should be hammered with the left hand, not played with the right.

# Solo y Triste

Mel Agen

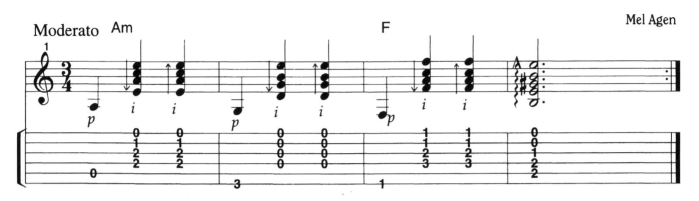

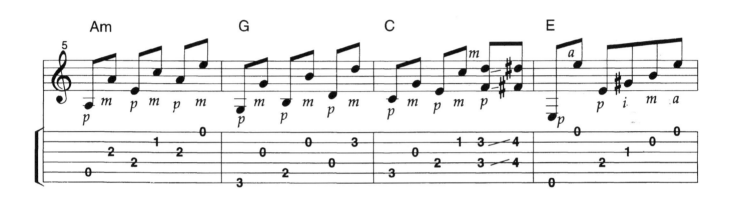

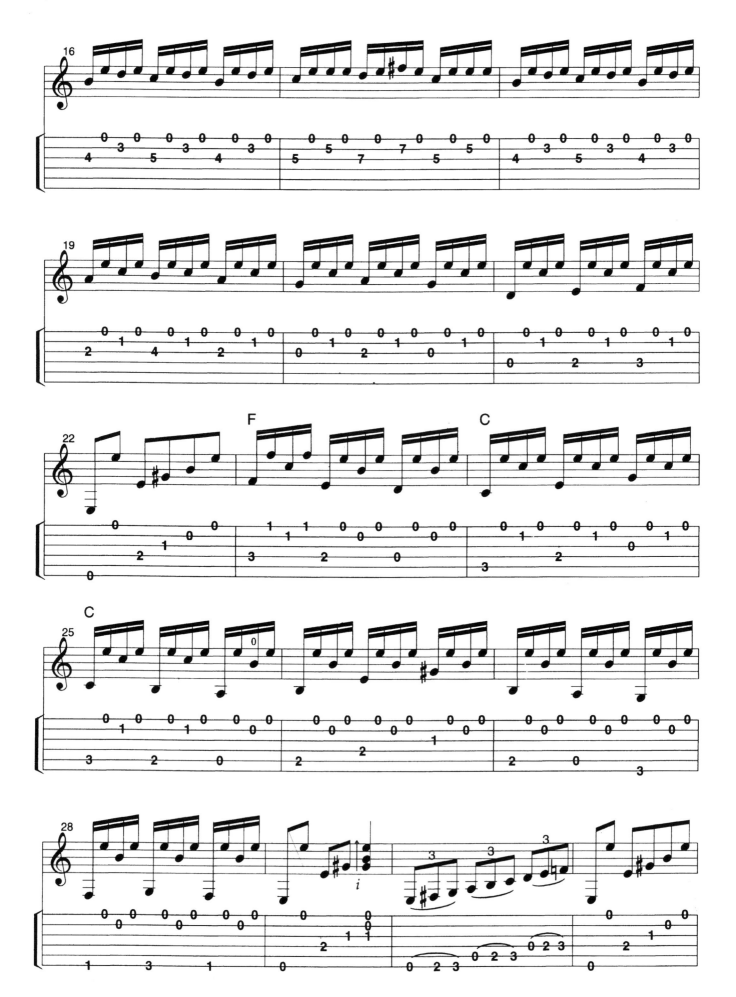

18

Play piece twice = 3 min.

19

# Alegrias in A

*Mel Agen*

Play entire piece twice = 3 min.

# Cantineros

Bartender or owner's favorite song

*Mel Agen*

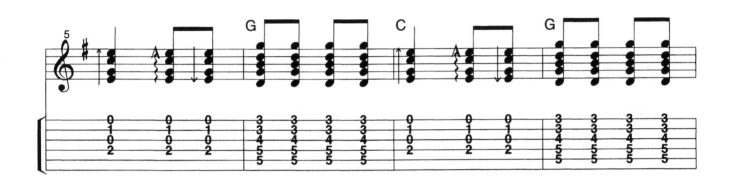

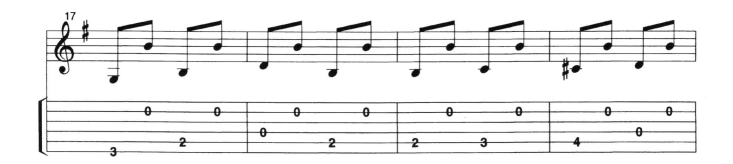

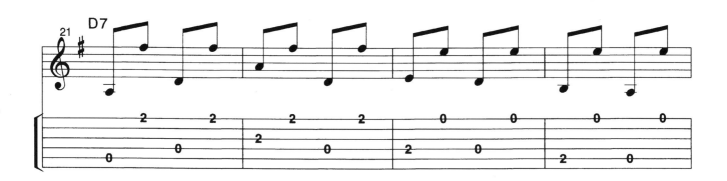

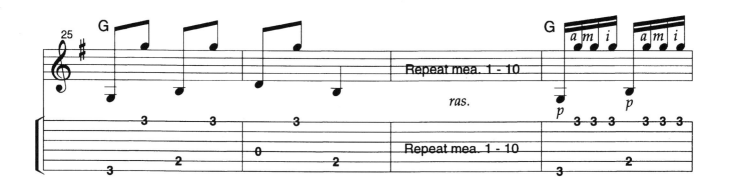

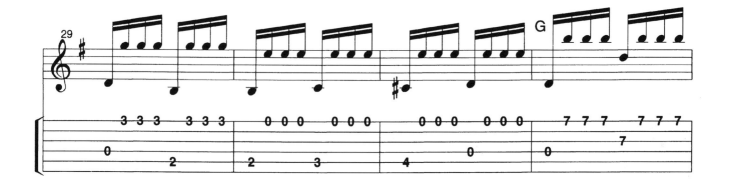

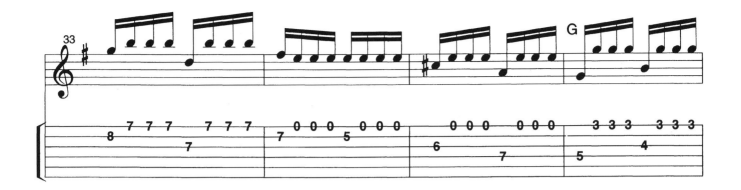

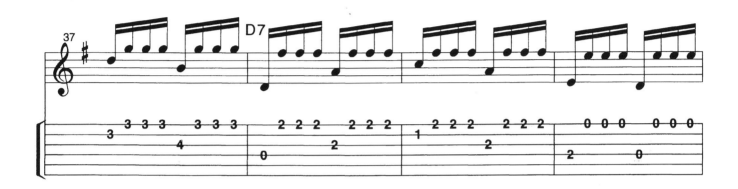

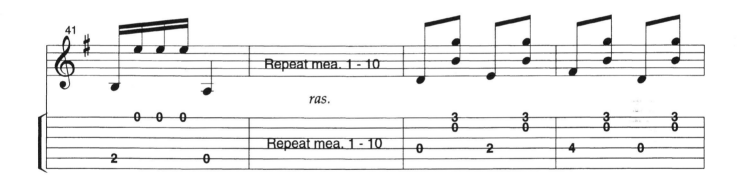

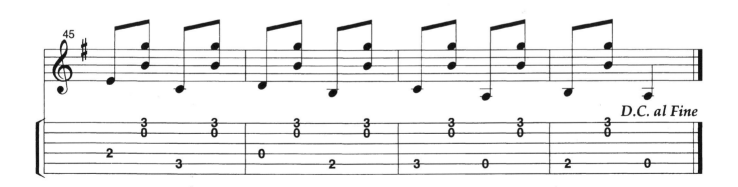

# The Saracens Dance

Note the use of minor chords in the rasqueado.

Mel Agen

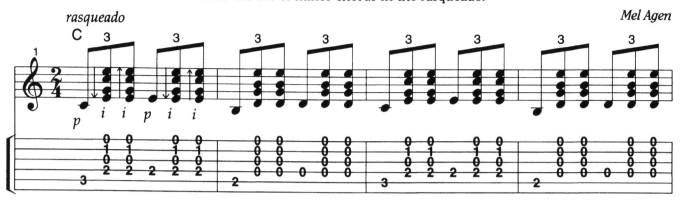

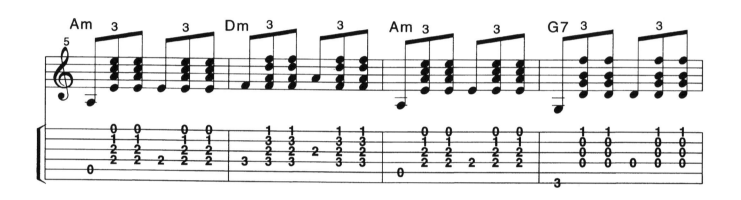

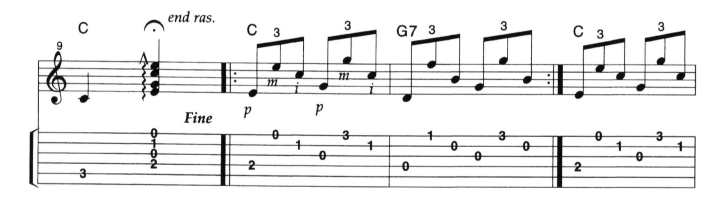

27

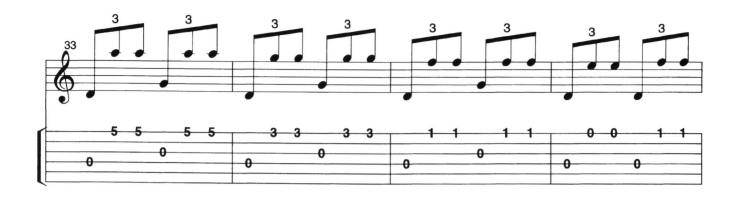

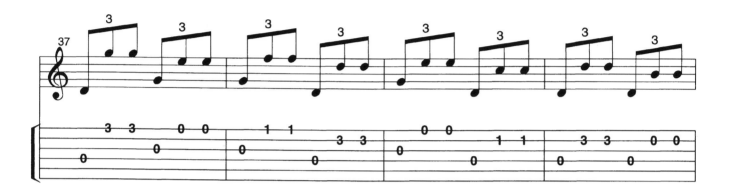

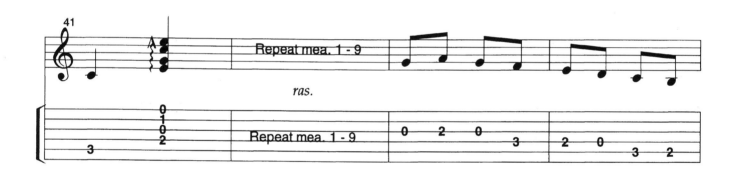

Repeat mea. 1 - 9

ras.

D.C. al Fine

Play through twice, then D.C. al Fine = 2:45 min.

# Idioma Musical

## Moorish Dance

*Mel Agen*

B7 style chord moves down
fingerboard on this page.

D.S. al Fine